You are a

Barnabas

to me

Vicky Litmer

truth
BOOKS

ISBN 10: 1-58427-389-5

ISBN 13: 978-1-58427-389-9

Guardian of Truth Foundation
CEI Bookstore
220 S. Marion St., Athens, AL 35611
1-855-49-BOOKS or 1-855-492-6657
www.CEIbooks.com

Table of Contents

You Are A Barnabas To Me

Being a child of God is the most marvelous blessing there could ever be! When the world becomes a strange and fearsome place, as it often does, Christians know that we simply need to *"cease striving, and know that I am God"* (Psa. 46:10). He is in control and there is nothing we truly need to fear.

But sometimes we also need our brethren to remind us of Him, to calm us when we're overwhelmed, to pick us up when we are low, and to simply be there for us. In Acts 4:36 we meet a man named Barnabas who, in this particular passage, sold land and gave the money to the apostles for distribution among needy saints. We see Barnabas in many different places in

Scripture, preaching the gospel and taking a bold
stand for Christ. We also see in the above passage that
the name Barnabas means "Son of Encouragement."
What a blessing he must have been to those early
Christians, and what a blessing it is for each of us to
have those encouragers among us!

I would like to acknowledge some who are a
"Barnabas" to me, simply to let you know that you
encourage me, and others, beyond measure.

Parents of Small Children

To you parents of small children – you are a Barnabas to me! How well I remember those days of interrupted, distracted, and often non-existent worship! How well I remember beating a path from the auditorium to the cry room and back again, sometimes several times. And I remember thinking, "Why am I even doing this?" Please know that your efforts are well worth the time and the frustration. That fussy, tired, whiny, and yes, sometimes even bratty child is being trained, being taught, by your perseverance and faithfulness. Every worship service brings him one step closer to learning the respect he needs to show when in God's house, and, before you realize it, he himself will be worshipping. It encourages me to see the children giving their little nickels and dimes

into the basket, hearing their off-key voices "singing" (whether at the proper time or not!), and hearing a noisy "Amen!" at the end of a prayer. And I even love hearing their inappropriate fussing (sometimes in chorus!), because they are *there.*

God bless you parents who realize the importance of training your child in the way he/she should go. God bless you for realizing that being at each service of the Lord's church, whether at regular times or gospel meetings, is teaching them. God bless you for realizing that bringing them to work days of your congregation is additional training. God bless you for showing them that nothing is more important to you than God and the opportunities to worship and serve Him. They may become tired; they may miss bedtimes; they may not understand the importance of it themselves. But those of us around you do, and we appreciate you so much.

Bless you for your efforts. You are living up to the command that the Lord gave in Deuteronomy 6:6-7, *"And these words, which I am commanding you today, shall be on your hearts; and you shall teach them diligently to your sons and shall talk of them when you sit in your house, and when you walk by the way, and when you lie down, and when you rise up."* Oh, yes, you are a Barnabas to me!

Widows and Widowers

Faithful widows and widowers – you are a Barnabas to me. I look and see you sitting in your pews, sometimes next to another in your situation, but never again with that companion you chose for life. My heart breaks for the sorrow you have endured in losing your mate, but at the same time it humbles me. I know how I am strengthened on a daily basis by my faithful spouse. There are so many times when I become sad, weary, and weak; but my husband's support and example bring me up to a better place, a more spiritual place.

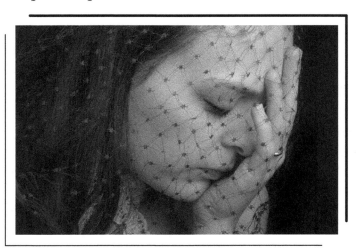

Seeing you without your partner gives me pause. It makes me think of how I would feel in the same situation, if tomorrow my husband were no longer with me. Being joined with a good spouse for so many years makes me feel as though we truly are intertwined emotionally, mentally, and spiritually. The very thought of his absence from my life causes me to shudder, and it also causes me to reflect on my relationship with him. Such an idea should cause each of us to think: "Would I speak harshly to him if I knew this was our last day together?" "Would I roll my eyes at something she said if I knew I wouldn't hear her voice again?" "Would I find this subject worthy of an argument if I knew that tomorrow we would be separated forever?" Would I nag? Would I yell? Would I complain? I know we could each add question after question to this list. The fact is, we should be respectful, loving, and kind to our mates each and every day, even when we disagree, for none of us (even you young married ones) are guaranteed seventy, sixty, or fifty years together, nor even one more day. Those of you who have lost your husbands and wives make me remember that marriage is not a license to treat my spouse with rudeness, sarcasm, or anger.

Beyond that, I am so very encouraged by your faithfulness in your attendance and service to God, even without that additional support from your mate. It makes me remember Hebrews 11:4, *"He being dead yet speaks."* Those years of uplifting and edifying one another to greater service continue to bear fruit even after one has gone on. I cannot imagine that you would even think of giving up now, after the blessing of so many years with a strong companion; and yet I have no doubt that the sorrow and loneliness can be sometimes overwhelming. Please know that you are a stellar example to all of us who are watching. You are a blessing to those of us who have been married for a good while, to those who are young in their marriages, and to those who will one day contemplate marriage. May we all strive to emulate your wonderful examples in faithfulness to your spouse, but most importantly, in faithfulness to God.

Your example causes me to reflect on God's plan for marriage. Seeing couples who have weathered life's storms brings to my mind Matthew 19:5-6, *"For this cause a man shall leave his father and mother, and shall cleave to his wife; and the two shall become one flesh. Consequently they are no longer two, but one flesh. What therefore God has joined together, let no man separate."* We live in a time when marriages are entered into thoughtlessly and ended just as thoughtlessly. I have actually heard couples planning marriage say, "Well, if it doesn't work out, we can always get a divorce." I look at you faithful widows and widowers and know that was never even the slightest consideration when you married your spouse. You knew then, as you took your vows, that it was "until death do you part." I pray that our young people also remember this when they plan marriage. The times are scary in this arena, with quickie divorces and same-sex marriages, and those who advocate such things never once considering the words of the One Who created marriage in the first place. I know you had hard times in your marriage, for we all do. Yet you leaned upon your Lord and His wisdom to help you through; and I'm sure that once your life's companion is gone, the rough patches are hardly remembered while the good times become your precious memories.

It humbles me to see how God helps you through your sorrow, for even in the midst of grief, your desire is to be with your brethren in worship and in service to Him. To my shame, I know that I have not prayed for you as often as I should have in the past; but I am determined to do better in the future. I know that one day my husband or I will leave the other, and I would certainly hope that others would pray for us, not just in the immediate aftermath but even as the years go by. Having lost both my parents and my brother, I know that the pain continues on, maybe not as acutely but every bit as real. As you enter into the church building with your smiles and your heads held high, I know it is through God's powerful love that you are managing as well as you are. And if your spouse was a faithful Christian, I know your plan is to be eternally with him or her in heaven. While it must be incredibly hard here, you know that *"...the sufferings of this present time are not worthy to be compared with the glory that is to be revealed in us"* (Rom. 8:18). God bless you all – you are very much a Barnabas to me!

Those with an Unbelieving Spouse

To you who are faithful in service to God even though you have an unbelieving spouse – you are a Barnabas to me. This situation would bring some very unique and difficult hardships, depending on how your mate handles your faithfulness. I know there are those whose spouses are very supportive, even making sure you can worship on the Lord's Day when you travel. But I also know that there are others who begrudge any time you spend with the saints for any reason. What obstacles can come up in situations like these! I know that being married to a faithful Christian makes my own Christian walk so much easier. It makes me wonder how I would handle it if my husband gave me a hard time whenever I wanted to worship. Would I square my shoulders and set off despite the consequences? Or would I find myself giving in a little here and there just to keep things peaceful?

I am certain there are many times you wish you could share your faith with your mate – both the joys and the difficulties that come with being a Christian. But that is an area where your paths do not meet. I once read an article by a devout Christian woman who had married an unbeliever. She wrote of standing before the preacher during the wedding ceremony and both of them repeating their vows. And then she said, "Neither one of us had any idea what that meant." Of course, I understand that young couples often do not *truly* understand what comes with "for richer or poorer," "in sickness and in health," but especially "for better or worse" (worse can be pretty bad!). But in her case she was talking about the conflicts that came about because of her faith and his lack of it. She often had to entertain his friends and family whose lifestyles came in direct conflict with her beliefs. By the same token, he often wanted to plan activities with her in which she refused to participate because of her beliefs. And many times he was angry because she refused to miss any services of the Lord's church, so he always had to plan around them. But worst of all, their children were affected by the example of their father and also chose to walk with the world. I must say, that article gave me pause. How hard would that be, day in and day out? How hard it would be to remember 2 Thessalonians 3:12, *"But as for you, brethren, do not grow weary of doing good."* Yet she realized that she had made those serious vows before God and was determined to live up to them as best she could – just as I see you doing.

I have a friend who is married to a non-Christian. We were together at a wedding shower once where we had to write advice to the future bride. Mine was to buy white appliances, because I was stuck with a coppertone colored stove and refrigerator for nearly twenty years! But hers was "Marry a Christian." And what so amazed me about this was that her husband attended most of the services with her, even gospel meetings, and seemed to dearly love the members. But he still had never accepted the Lord and rendered his obedience to Him. They still could not totally share that mutual faith. I am sure she is not alone in her advice to marry a believer. Young Christians, please listen and learn from the experiences of those in this situation and make your mind up now that this will not be your path.

I look at those of you who deal with this with admiration and amazement, praising God for your determination, knowing that you are striving to serve Him in the face of difficulties I cannot truly understand. Please know that you are in my prayers, and I am sure in the prayers of many others, for it will be your fine example that may one day bring your unbelieving spouse to the Lord. And that would be an encouragement to us all! You are truly a Barnabas to me!

You Are a Barnabas to Me.

Faithful Divorced Christians

Our times are very distressing when it comes to marriage and divorce. Statistics show that nearly 50% of all marriages will end in divorce, a sad reflection on the behavior and attitudes of present-day society. And while you would certainly expect that the church would be immune to such worldly thinking and practice, this is unfortunately not the case. So to all of you faithful Christians who find yourself in this category, I emphatically say that you are a Barnabas to me!

When we all got married, we made vows that included, "Until death do we part" (or some variation of that phrase). That is because marriage is intended to be just that – a lifelong commitment between a man and a woman. I do remember people telling me when I was engaged that I could "always get a divorce if it didn't work out." However, those were worldly people with whom I worked – not a single Christian gave me that terrible advice.

But when we look at the church today, we see many members who have been through the heartache of divorce through no fault of their own. I can't begin to imagine the grief you suffered when you discovered your spouse had betrayed you and your vows to be with someone else. I know that you shed countless tears, finding yourself in a position you never thought would be yours. I try to put myself in your place and know that, at some point, you must have felt rejected and worthless due to the actions of the one to whom you pledged your life. How devastating it must have been to find yourself in this unthinkable position!

And yet, never have you faltered in your walk with God. On the contrary, you embraced Him and your brethren more closely. You sought the wise counsel of the elders and other godly ones of your congregation to help you think clearly in making proper and biblically sound decisions. You used your church family to help hold you up when you felt you couldn't carry on and, if you have children, to comfort them when you were unable to even comfort yourself. You found the faith to carry you through and the strength that only God can provide His hurting children. Your brethren watched in awe as you managed to pull yourself through that mire and create a new life for yourself and your kids.

Whenever children are involved, it is so difficult to put things behind you and march on. You find yourself having to share custody and to come face to face with your ex-spouse on a regular basis. So you strive to find the balance you will all need to handle that unfaithful one's ungodliness while still teaching your young ones the ways of God. It especially sickens me how one who had been a Christian and cheated on his/her spouse suddenly tries to demonize that innocent spouse and justify the ungodly actions taken that ended the marriage. Oh, the feelings of anger and unfairness you must fight on a regular basis! God bless you with the struggles many of us can only imagine!

If your spouse committed fornication, you know that marriage can still be in your future (Matt. 19:9). I've known some who vowed never to marry again, lest such betrayal happen a second time. I can certainly understand that caution and the desire to avoid even the possibility of feeling such deep pain again. But I also pray, should remarriage happen for you, that you find the joy, peace, and commitment you deserve and should be able to expect from your mate.

But there are also terribly sad cases of spouses divorcing their husband or wife for reasons other than fornication. In this most difficult circumstance, I have been humbled by your acceptance of the fact you can never marry again. You look to God's Word with such understanding and love, knowing that He has your best interests always in mind, that He is never wrong in His commands, and that He always loves you and knows best. Accepting singleness and celibacy as the scriptural outcome of someone else's ungodliness glorifies God in a way that words never could. Such love and devotion to our Lord is a living testimony to your brethren, to your children, and to the world. Your life truly is a spiritual sacrifice to our Creator (Rom. 12:1).

So to you, my divorced brothers and sisters, who continue to stand strong in the Lord and in the power of His might, I say to you with all my heart that you are a Barnabas to me!

Faithful Single Adults

Faithful single adults – you are a Barnabas to me. It would be so easy to let the cares and concerns that you have to handle distract you from your walk with God. Yet I see you using this time in your life to do more than ever for the Lord. You never allow the fact that you are single to be an excuse for being less for God.

You work a full week, yet you are ever faithful in your attendance

> *It would be so easy to let the cares and concerns that you have to handle distract you from your walk with God.*

in pretty much every aspect of the work of the church. I see you in the regular worship services. I see you each night of a gospel meeting. I see you at any group meetings the congregation has. I see you going around to visitors, introducing yourself and making them feel welcome to our services. I see you teaching classes. I see your absolute involvement in the work of our congregation, even though you have so much that could keep you away.

To me, most single people are interesting, whether they are single by choice or by circumstance. I suppose because you have more discretionary time than married people with children, you seem to be busy and engaged in so many things. I see your pursuits – travel, culture, sports, self-improvement, home improvement, gardening, music, reading, and a host of other things that bring you personal enjoyment. And while I know that sometimes having only one income can make things tight, you seem to be so well rounded in your various pursuits. But you also show that these pursuits have their place and do not deter you from the most important thing – serving God and your brethren. I have seen many singles become "Go to work, go home, and sit in front of the tube" people. I don't see that in you. What a great example! Christians should be those who shine in the world and are joyful in any circumstance. By watching you in your secular activities, I know that you are also growing in your spiritual life. It is something you take very seriously; I know that because you shine for your brethren as well.

To many in the world, being single is synonymous with living for worldly pleasure since you have no ties at home to keep you from them. So often your co-workers can make it difficult for you to say no to their invitations to ungodly places and events; yet you are focused on the eternal goal and will not allow anyone or anything to take you away from the One you truly love. You use your opportunities to the glory of God, not for your own personal amusement. You make me look into my own heart to see if I would have the same self motivation and drive that you have; I hope that I would, especially seeing how well you edify your brethren. You are a Barnabas to me!

"Single by Conviction" Christians

It seems that many of us are not happy unless every unmarried person we know has been "paired up" with someone—after all, who isn't happier as a couple instead of a single, right? We want to introduce them to all the wonderful Christians we know who (we are certain) would be perfect for them, fulfill them, and be the one with whom they can grow old. While it's true that sometimes we may be successful in our matchmaking, there are many more times when it just isn't going to happen. And, of course, we know that simply because two people are Christians does not necessarily make them personally compatible.

So, to you unmarried Christians who have stayed single because you haven't found the right Christian to marry, you are an exceptional Barnabas to me!

I know many of you have dated non-Christians, even becoming emotionally serious in at least one of these relationships, to the point of considering a proposal of marriage. But your conviction has been that you will only marry someone who has accepted the Lord wholeheartedly and put Him on in baptism. How tempting it would be to convince yourself that your spiritual differences would improve after marriage, or certainly after children, and that he or she would eventually obey the gospel. We all know of those situations, where after many years of marriage an unbelieving spouse suddenly, or finally, committed him/herself to the Lord.

But there are also those on the other side of that coin, where the spiritual differences became chasms, points of argument and irritation, where no amount of explanation could relieve the tension that had built up. We have seen those faithful Christians grieve over the burden they carry on a daily basis, and we grieve with them. They are, in essence, a divided household, with the unbeliever sometimes even offering to start going to services with the believer if they would just "choose another religion." They simply don't, or won't, get it. There can be no compromises when it comes to our faith.

And so, because you realize that marriage is for life, that even the strongest of Christian marriages are not without difficulties, and that the best mate you could have would share your love of the Lord, you have said "no" to the unbeliever. You know that you have already made your greatest commitment, and you have chosen to live a single and celibate life rather than risk embracing someone who could cause your commitment to falter (2 Cor. 6:14). It is not that you don't want to be married; you just want to go to heaven more. This is a decision for which people in the world, and sadly some in the church, would question and even condemn you.

So you use your time and talents for His glory, praying that the right Christian man or woman will one day come your way, but accepting the fact that it may never happen. Are you angry or bitter? It sure doesn't appear that way. You seem to accept whatever His Will to be in all circumstances and know that eternity will be worth whatever you must sacrifice here (Rom. 8:18). How pleased He must be to see your strength and dedication to the church for which His Son died. How blessed your brethren are to be able to see your light shine in praise and devotion to Him (Matt. 5:16). You are without question a Barnabas to me!

Christians Who "Adopt" Other Christians

What a blessing it is to live near family! How nice to be able to pick up the phone to call parents and siblings to come over for a spur-of-the-moment cookout, to run over to visit a favorite aunt, or to meet up with a cousin for lunch and shopping. It is an extra-special blessing to be able to worship with our family members. How fun to let the little ones sit by grandma and grandpa during services and go to Bible classes with their cousins. Many take these situations for granted because it has always been this way — they have never known what it is to have no extended family nearby. It is not that way for all of us.

Nowadays we live in a very transient world. Many jobs require us to relocate as they dictate, and if we choose not to do that — well, we may have to start searching for a new job, which may also require moving. It's a very common occurrence for families to move to unfamiliar cities and have to seek out a new congregation with which to worship. While, as a preacher's family, we have obviously never had to seek out a new church, I do know what it is like to look out at a congregation of unfamiliar faces and feel a little bit lost and, well, homesick.

Additionally, there are those who just don't have a lot of family, period; some whose families are so dysfunctional, or so hostile toward them because of their Christianity, that they have found it practically impossible to be around them. We all know of older couples who are childless, or whose children have moved away, and widows and widowers in that same situation. These people are pretty much on their own, family-wise, and that can be a lonely circumstance.

> *To you Christians who have taken us and others under your wing and sought to lessen our feelings of displacement, you are a Barnabas to me!*

However, at least in each congregation with which we have worked, there have been those who reached out to the ones longing for far-away home and family or who have no family at all, and decided to do something about it. To you Christians who have taken

us and others under your wing and sought to lessen
our feelings of displacement, you are a Barnabas to me!

Often you wonderful, hospitable people are the
very ones who have much of your own families
nearby. Yet rather than close your eyes to those of the
congregation who are on their own, family-wise, you
open your heart and look about you. You see them,
and you have so much empathy and love in your
hearts that there is no way you would leave them on
their own.

Knowing that distance and money can make it
impossible for some families to always go "home"
for the holidays, and knowing that for others there
is simply no place for them to go anyway, you
"adopt" these people and include them in your own
family celebrations. You don't worry about seating
arrangements, matching place settings, spotless
corners, or overcrowding. You have that amazing
"the more, the merrier" outlook. Your families accept
that there will always be extra places at the table
and they appreciate you for that. You understand
that those of us without nearby families need you to
become our family.

I can assure you that the ones you include don't
care if they are eating off of the finest bone china or
paper plates, if they sit around a huge and spacious
table or prop their dish on their lap. It is just such
a blessing and a thrill to be considered "part of the
family," for that day. At one congregation we were
with, even though we were only a couple of hours
away from our families and saw them on every
holiday, there was an older couple who refused to let

us spend Christmas Eve alone, even buying us small gifts so we could feel even more a part of everything. But lest you think it is always older folks who do this, I also know a young couple in their 20's with several small home-schooled children, who practiced this same type of hospitality.

So, to those of you who set this beautiful example of love and inclusion, who fulfill John's exhortation to love one another "in deed and in truth" (1 John 3:18), thank you! Thank you for enlarging your view of what it means to be family. To you I can say beyond doubt and with a full heart, you are a Barnabas to me!

Whole-Hearted Worshipers

To all of you whole-hearted worshipers out there – you are a Barnabas to me! It thrills my heart to see you interested and involved in all aspects of the worship service. Your devotion to our Lord and His church is an inspiration to me, and I'm sure to everyone else. We all know that the Lord authorized five acts of worship. You perform each one with all of your heart, and it is obvious.

To you hearty singers – thank you! Singing can affect the whole mood of a worship service, so those of you who sing with enthusiasm are very much appreciated. When I was a (much) younger preacher's

wife, an older sister in Christ said to me, "Some
people sing like they think God is deaf." I really didn't
know how to respond to that, other than to give her
a weak smile and wonder if she was talking about
me. But I know how I would reply to her today: "I
don't believe for a second that God is displeased with
spirited singing, especially since He commanded it."
I have visited a number of congregations over the
years where many of the members barely opened
their mouths to sing, nor did they crack open a song
book. The results were always lackluster and certainly
not edifying to anyone. On the other hand, I've been
to many congregations where the singing practically
raised the roof, and it is always amazing! In which
way is God most glorified? That is not to say that we
have to scream our songs, but I believe the whole
purpose behind the command to sing is to uplift
ourselves and those around us, as well as praising
Him. We are to sing with spirit and understanding (1
Cor. 14:15); we are to do everything for edification (1
Cor. 14:26); we are to teach and admonish one another
through song (Col. 3:16). When I hear you singing
with gusto to the Lord, I know it is important to you.
The Lord never asked for only good singers to sing,
or only the ones who enjoy singing. It is for all His
children to hold up His name in psalms, hymns, and
spiritual songs. He doesn't care if some are off-key;
He just wants you to sing! And isn't it sweet to hear
the little voices joining in as they get old enough to
sing some of the words? Your efforts are teaching
them, as well as visitors, babes in Christ, and seasoned
Christians, what it means to praise God in song. You
show that a mechanical instrument of music is not

needed if we are willing to use the instrument God gave to us. You whole-hearted singers of spiritual songs – you are a Barnabas to me!

Song Leaders

In the same vein, you enthusiastic song leaders are a Barnabas to me. Without you, the congregation would not be able to sing at its best. You are always prepared with your song numbers in advance, and sometimes even try to coordinate them with the sermon topic. You choose a mixture of slower and faster songs, which makes a nice change of pace. You sometimes even preface the start of a song with a few words about it to help us focus our minds on the meaning. You strive to make sure the congregation keeps up with the tempo, which I am sure is not always an

easy thing to do. And with all this going on, your singing is always spirited. I know that you spend time beforehand preparing for this task, which in the past, I have certainly taken for granted. And I love that sometimes you are even willing to lead an unfamiliar song, knowing that it may feel as if you're singing a solo until we can catch on – but we will catch on and have another wonderful song to use in worship and praise to our Creator. We can never have too many songs to sing! And I know that on our singing nights, some who lead songs are stepping out of their comfort zones in doing so. Please know that you make my heart proud! It is a function that does not come easily to everyone, but it is wonderful to see you using this avenue to help yourself grow. In so doing, you are helping me grow. You are appreciated, song leaders – you are a Barnabas to me!

Bible Openers

To those who use your Bible throughout worship service – you are a Barnabas to me! This may seem like a strange thing to mention, but I have been to places where hardly anyone bothered to follow along with Scripture or even brought a Bible with them. I have often admonished my Bible class students when they have forgotten to bring their Bibles to class by telling them, "When you go to English class, you take your English book. When you go to science class, you take your science book. When you come to Bible class, you bring your Bible." I don't know how anyone could follow along in worship or Bible study without using a Bible. It is so satisfying to me to hear the pages rustling as people turn to the various passages that are mentioned. And I know that in this electronic age,

 some people don't have actual pages to turn. But you have that little device with you and are using it as an aid in your study. You follow along with the

content of the sermon and search the Scriptures to make sure that the things being taught are true, just like the noble Bereans of Acts 17:11. Much error has entered into the religious world over the centuries because people simply accepted the teachings of others without looking into it themselves. You consider Hosea 4:6 where God said, *"My people are destroyed for lack of knowledge,"* and refuse to let that be

> I appreciate that you take your Christianity so seriously as to know you never can stop learning.

your case. I know that there are some who even take notes so that they can continue to study at home. I appreciate that you take your Christianity so seriously as to know you never can stop learning. Even the imprisoned Paul asked for parchments to be brought to him so he could continue studying – and he was an apostle! I see you striving to be like that and it means so much to your brethren. Please know that you are a Barnabas to me!

Those Who Lead in Public Prayer

I want to thank the men who lead the congregation in public prayer – you are such a Barnabas to me! I know it can't be an easy thing to pray on behalf of a whole group of listening people, yet you are able to touch my heart, and I am sure the hearts of many others, as you approach the Throne for us. It is obvious by the ease of your prayers that you pray regularly and that you are a friend of God. Many of you write down the names of those mentioned in

the announcements as being sick or having some other special needs and make sure we all include them as you direct our minds. Praying in public does not mean that a man has a special gift of oratory or the ability to move people to vast emotional heights, although that may be the case sometimes. But it does show a humble spirit

and a respect for God and His church that brings me
to my (figurative) knees whenever you address Him.
Even the simplest prayers, when they are heartfelt, can
bring tears to my eyes, and I know they are pleasing to
the Lord.

You always remember the purpose of our prayer at
your appointed time. By that I mean that the opening
prayer encompasses many things pertaining to the
congregation and beyond our walls, the Lord's Supper
prayers are always specific to His body and blood
given for our cleansing, the closing prayer is generally
brief and sends us off with supplications for His
blessings and the safety of those of us praying along.
You give thought to your prayers and take this act of
worship very seriously, and for that I am grateful.

I appreciate it so much when you spend time in
praise and thanksgiving to the Lord. So often I tend
to rush through those parts of my prayers to get to
the "request" portion; and even though my requests
are not always just for me and mine, I realize through
your example that time and thought need to be taken
for those very important aspects of prayer as well. You
make me remember the words to the song, "Worthy
Art Thou," when we sing, "Worthy of praise is Christ
my Redeemer; Worthy of wisdom, glory, and power;
Worthy of earth and heaven's thanksgiving; Worthy
art Thou, Worthy art Thou." If such words don't send
a thrill to our very core, I can't imagine what would!

As the wife of a preacher, I find the requests made
on our behalf so very humbling. Hardly a service
goes by in which one or both of us are not mentioned
in some regard, and I have to say it is an awesome

> Hardly a service goes by in which one or both of us are not mentioned in some regard, and I have to say it is an awesome thing to know that a whole congregation of people is approaching God about us

thing to know that a whole congregation of people is approaching God about us. I know it is because of my husband's more public functions in the church and his work on its behalf; but I have absolutely no doubt that you are also approaching Him privately on behalf of so many others in the congregation who need prayers and that He is listening to those as well. You are a wonderful example to me and others of the attitudes we should have toward prayer, toward one another, and toward the elders who lead this church. Having been to places where prayers tended to be little more than rote recitations with very little time or forethought given to them, I have to tell you that I appreciate your efforts so much. You all are a Barnabas to me!

Generous Contributors

To you generous contributors of money each first day of the week, you are a Barnabas to me! Now I have absolutely no idea who gives what, outside of my own family, but I know that many of you are giving significantly of your means. I know this because I see how many families we have and how much the contribution is each week. When you factor in spouses and children, it is obvious that we have many who are serious about this particular act of worship. Whenever this generosity is shown, the local congregation is able to accomplish so many things that it couldn't hope to undertake otherwise. Many help in the support of several gospel preachers all over the country and the world. You make the purchase of curriculum for Bible classes possible. The congregation is able to offer benevolence to many saints who have had unexpected expenses or have fallen on hard times because the money was there. I could go on and on about the scriptural ways that the church's funds are being used – and it's all due to your understanding of the Lord's instructions to give of your means and to be a cheerful giver. I certainly can't imagine a single one of you grumbling when you write your check each week. And I truly appreciate those of you who leave your contribution behind when you travel or make it up when you return.

Being the type of giver the Lord wants requires making a decision to set aside a certain amount specifically for Him and refusing to allow anything to interfere with that. We live in expensive times and children insist on growing out of their clothes and wanting more and more food to eat! But you remember that wonderful verse in Luke 6:38: *"Give and it will be given to you; good measure, pressed down, shaken together, running over, they will pour into your lap. For by your standard of measure it will be measured to you in return."* He promised this and you believe it. Oh, generous brethren, it is such a pleasure to be part of a congregation that understands God's teachings and promises in this area. You are a Barnabas, not only to me, but to all those who benefit from your generosity!

Teachers of Children's Classes

Diligent teachers of children's classes – you are a Barnabas to me! It takes such time and care to do a good job as a teacher, and from what I have seen you do an exemplary job. I know that you are busy. Many of you have full-time jobs outside of the home, and many of you have an even more full-time job raising children. Some of you actually work at teaching other people's children, and some of you work the same hours teaching your own. So I know that your time is extremely limited, yet you accept the incredible responsibility of teaching.

Most churches put a great emphasis upon the children's teaching program. If our children do not learn as much as possible now, there will be huge gaps in their understanding of Scripture and the way it all fits together later. The primary focus for you, and every teacher in the congregation, is to impart to your students God's plan for mankind, His wisdom, His instructions for us, and ultimately to help teach those students how to get to heaven.

James 3:1 tells us, *"Let not many of you become teachers, my brethren, knowing that as such we shall incur a stricter judgment."* I do not believe that this applies only to teachers of adult classes. Teaching the children of Christians is incredibly important and should never be entered into lightly. Even though the littlest ones can't learn things that are very abstract or complex, you teachers are setting the foundation for their future learning when they will be able to grasp those concepts. It is wonderful to see the small children anxious to go class and to see them come from their classes excited to have been there. It is easy to see the painstaking care and effort that you have put in to making sure your students grasp the material.

Teaching children can be tough. And one of the reasons it can be tough is because . . . they are children. They go through their various stages of growth and maturity which can be, in turn, both entertaining and frustrating. Over the years I have taught pretty much every age up through middle school. I know what it is like to tell the little ones the thrilling story of our Lord rising from the tomb and living again, only to have one of them tell me about the dead bird he saw on his driveway that morning. I have had (what I believed to be) an exciting presentation to a group of middle school children flop because one of the boys wanted to show off his charm (?) and wit (??) to the girls in the class. There are students who have trouble staying focused; the ones who talk too much, the ones who never have their Bible or their homework, and the list could go on. And sometimes you have to become more firm than you might like in order for them to realize the significance of Bible class and that you will not allow the class to be disrupted or disrespected.

But I have found those issues to be exceptions rather than rules. Children at congregations where they have been diligently taught have such knowledge and understanding of the stories and lessons found in Scripture. And while I know that most of that is because of their wonderful and godly parents, it is also because of their wonderful and godly teachers. Satan desperately wants these children, and your efforts will help keep them from him. Yes, it is a huge commitment, but the time you spend teaching the children is well spent. I will always be thankful for the teachers who taught my kids when they were growing up. Bless you for your willingness to take on the role of Bible class teacher. You are a Barnabas to me!

Teachers of Adult Bible Classes

Teachers of adult Bible classes, you are a Barnabas to me! A teacher who has a thorough understanding of his material and presents it in such a way as to help his class grow in the knowledge of the truth is a tremendous asset to any congregation. And while teaching children takes a great deal of study and preparation, an adult Bible class takes that study to a whole different level.

An adult Bible class is an interesting thing. The class is usually made up of people from various religious backgrounds; some may be brand new Christians and have very little of the foundation that even the elementary students who grew up going to Bible classes have already attained. Some students may have studied the Scriptures all their lives and have a tremendous amount of knowledge. The Bible class teacher is in a position of needing to make the study understandable to those with less knowledge while at the same time keeping the more knowledgeable students involved. It can be a difficult tightrope to walk in that regard, plus there is the need to be able to answer any questions that come up with sound reasoning from the Scriptures. But, again, as I reflect on my time in the church and all the Bible classes through which I have sat, I have always respected a teacher who will say, "I don't know the answer to that question, but I will find out." None of us knows everything, but given the time, the answers can be found.

> " ... I have always respected a teacher who will say, "I don't know the answer to that question, but I will find out." None of us knows everything, but given the time, the answers can be found.

Another thing that has impressed me about so many teachers of adult Bible classes has been your ability to present your material. It takes a special skill to be able to do that. I have had teachers who knew their subject backward and forward, yet their ability to impart that knowledge fell short. And while I do believe that the students have a responsibility to focus and follow along in any study, still it is important that teachers show the class that the subject matter is also interesting to them. Teachers of adult Bible classes, your love of the Word and your willingness to study and share what you learn with the rest of us makes you a Barnabas to me!

Generous Givers of Time

Those of you who give so generously of your time to the local congregation and brethren, you are a Barnabas to me! I have the great privilege of knowing so many brethren in so many congregations who take seriously the Lord's commands to love and help their brethren. Generous "do-gooders" truly show the spirit that the Scriptures teach us to have in passages such as 1 Peter 1:22, *"Since you have in obedience to the truth purified your souls for a sincere love of the brethren, fervently love one another from the heart."* Sincere and fervent love – that is what you show.

Everything that we do for the Lord's church is done voluntarily; and considering how much some do, it is an inspiring thing. I started to make a list of some of the various ways you step up, and I just kept thinking of more and more; yet I'm certain that I haven't even scratched the surface. As a matter of fact, I'm sure there is much of which I am not aware, for you do these things, not for personal acclaim or any type of glory, but because you love the church.

You spend much time preparing your classrooms, coming to the church building at times other than worship services just to run copies, decorate your rooms, look for craft ideas, etc. And you often bring your little ones along as you work, teaching them from your fine example.

The congregation I attend has a wonderful ladies' class that currently meets once a month, and while most women are very adept at teaching children's classes, it is different teaching adults. Yet there are many women who volunteer, sometimes nervously, for their turn to teach because they know it is important. The faithful ladies who participate never allow the class to deteriorate into a gossip session or a mere social time. I have been strengthened by you sisters who work so hard to make sure our ladies' classes are times of study and growth. I am certain that the same thing takes place in many local congregations.

> *Those of you who give so generously of your time to the local congregation and brethren, you are a Barnabas to me!*

Whenever there is an illness, a birth, or something of that nature, a meal list is prepared. I can't count the number of times I have found an email on my computer asking for people to sign up for a meal list, only to see that it was already filled before I got to it! And the meal lists for gospel meetings are always filled as well. I pray that is the case in all congregations of the Lord's people, for it is such a blessing.

There are those who diligently take their turns cleaning the church building, even some who live a long distance from the building. I have seen brethren stay late after Wednesday evening services to complete this duty. There are women who come early on Sunday mornings so they can take care of filling the Lord's Supper trays, again often with little ones in tow. There are sisters who plant flowers around the church buildings to show the beauty of God's wonderful creation. There are brothers who are often found mowing, weeding, and sprucing up the grounds at various times to keep them nice for all of us and visitors. First impressions are important.

There are those who open their homes regularly for Bible studies for anyone who would like to join them, and others who host times of fellowship and fun (which is not always easy depending upon the size of the congregation). There are several who organize activities throughout the year, sometimes for the whole congregation, sometimes specifically for the young people – and these are times which draw the local church even closer together.

My husband and I have often run into fellow Christians while visiting someone in the hospital or a nursing home. There are sisters who make it a point to take a few minutes in their children's Bible class to write cards to members needing encouragement. There are those who can always be counted on to show up for any scheduled work day and for door-to-door evangelistic endeavors. There are those who readily pick up those unable to drive themselves to worship services, and good sisters who routinely take some of the elderly ladies to lunch or to various appointments.

Of course, brethren can always be counted on when someone has a financial need. I know this because my family has been the recipient of the good hearts of brethren in this respect. Several years ago our daughter was very sick. We had to make two seven-hour (one-way) trips to Michigan for her surgeries, and our brethren were there for us. When the only words that could penetrate our fearful minds during this time were *cancer, lymph nodes, specialist, prognosis, and surgery*, the last thing we worried about was how much these trips would cost. But our brethren thought about it, and they inundated us with money, gas cards, gift cards, hotel points, the use of a van for our daughter's comfort, and even snacks and magazines for the trip. The most amazing thing about it was that we used the very last gift card as we were nearing home. I know that our family is not the only one that has been so blessed by loving, generous brethren.

Generous time givers, you are proactive as well as reactive in your good deeds. You never let your busy-ness, your young children, your jobs, or even your age, serve as excuses to hide your lights. You are figurative foot-washers, and you all make the church stronger. Each and every one of you is a Barnabas to me!

Faithful Parents of School-Aged Children

To all of the faithful parents of school-aged children, you are a Barnabas to me! How well I remember those first days of kindergarten with my children. The infant, toddler, and pre-school years had gone by so quickly and now my little ones were walking with their new clothes and new backpacks into their school years. I blinked once or twice, and they were walking down the aisle in their caps and gowns, receiving their diplomas. Whether your children go to public school, private school, or they are home schooled, these years are swift and replete with amazing changes. You can see those changes happening year by year, just by looking at their school pictures.

So here you are on this journey with your children. I can't say that I envy you. The world around us seems to be growing stranger, and more wicked, all the time. The challenges you face are so daunting, and now they are the challenges my own children face as they raise their children. I watch parents bring their elementary/middle school/high school children to services regularly, despite the fact that they need to get up early the next morning or have a pile of homework to finish. You recognize that their spiritual education takes precedence over their secular education. And one of the reasons is the very thing we just spoke of – the challenges all such families are facing.

Everything that is in the world is certainly in the schools. There is foul language (even at some very young ages), innuendo, immodesty, immoral lifestyles, and on and on we could go. Through the gargantuan efforts of faithful parents to raise their children well, you have provided your children with the tools they need to be victorious over the sin that surrounds them too often. How much we all wish we could enfold our children – cocoon them – from the filth of the world. But that is not possible, even for the home schooling parents. Children will be faced with difficult choices throughout their growing-up years, and the devotion of godly parents to the Lord, His church, and His Word will enable them to choose correctly.

Faithful parents of school-aged children, you are teaching them the place of extra-curricular activities in their lives, seeing to it that those activities never keep them from the most important aspect of their lives – the spiritual. I often see your kids coming to services in their athletic uniforms, having played as long as they could until it was time to go to Bible study. The coach was informed ahead of time and if he or she didn't like it, well . . . your child was leaving to worship God, and that was that. It's a hard decision but you are teaching them to make it.

Faithful parents, you are teaching your children to make wise friend choices. When my children started elementary school, for the first time they were making friends with kids who were not the children of my friends. I found that to be a little disquieting – another marker along the road of their development. I would often help out in their classrooms and see their interaction with others. Sometimes I would want to steer them toward another child who I preferred, or who seemed a better student, or whose mother I liked more. But I also realized that, unless their friend became a problem, I had little to say in the matter. Isn't that the independence we try to teach them? However, as a parent, you also have to watch to make sure there is no negative influence making its way into your child's life from poor friend choices. It makes me happy to see your children forming such good friendships with the other children in their home congregation. In this way, you know that they are with others whose parents are working just as hard as you to help their children get to heaven. While their school friends may be terrific kids, and you may not see any cause for alarm in these friendships, they still do not share the spiritual connection that we all need to have in those closest to us. Friendship is so important. Our friends are our confidants, our secret-keepers; they like us in spite of ourselves sometimes. So it is vitally important that these friends be those on the same righteous path as your children.

Faithful parents, you are teaching your children to make wise entertainment choices. This is another difficult issue these days, for ungodly entertainment is simply a remote control click, a mouse click, or an app away. As children grow, they want to be more independent. They want to go places with their friends. They want to be involved and included. You are bringing them up to say "no" when it is necessary, or to make alternative suggestions for activities. Again, this is where friendship with the kids of other Christians is so comforting. Everybody wants to be liked, and that is especially true of school-aged children. They are terrified of being considered un-cool, a nerd, weird. But you have taught them from an early age that their primary goal must be to please God, not other kids. I know (believe me, I know) how hard it is to tell your children that they cannot be included in certain school activities or recreational activities that "everybody else" is doing. Your firmness in this regard will have lasting value – eternal value.

Faithful parents, you are teaching your children to be polite, to respect authority, to work hard at their endeavors to tell the truth, and many other things that we wish all parents would teach their children. However, you are also teaching them that the father is the head of the home and works hard to support his family, that the mother submits to the father and keeps the home a pleasant place for them to be, and that you both love the Lord and are striving above all else to see that they get to heaven.

> "Train up a child in the way he should go, and when he is old he will not depart from it."

As a Bible teacher of school-aged children, it is wonderful when they know their Bible lessons, when they have obviously prepared for class. When they know the books of the Bible, ask intelligent questions, and learn to make application, it is thrilling for the teacher. I know it is because of the hard work you do with them at home. You love their souls and are teaching them to love them as well. You trust the words of Proverbs 22:6, *"Train up a child in the way he should go, and when he is old he will not depart from it."* You take seriously the command in Ephesians 6:4, *"Fathers, provoke not your children to wrath; but bring them up in the nurture and admonition of the Lord."* I specifically wanted to reference this verse because it is wonderful to see fathers working just as hard as mothers to save their children.

Faithful parents, you are in my prayers as you do the very best you can for your children. You are putting in the time, effort, and spiritual guidance they need to find their own way from this world to the next glorious one. We all know that the time we have to rear our children is very brief (even though some days seem very l-o-n-g). You are not wasting this time, all of you faithful fathers and mothers of school-aged children. I know there are days when you don't know what to do or you feel that you just don't have enough wisdom. But with the Lord's help, you are holding them up to His light and, little by little, helping them to find their own way to Him. You are a hero to them, and you are a Barnabas to me!

Teenage Christians

Our congregation is blessed with a fairly large group of teenagers. This is a wonderful thing for any congregation because young people add an exuberance and joy to everything that has to do with our worship and the times we gather at various places just to be together socially. To you teenagers, I want to say that you are a Barnabas to me!

You are at such an exciting time in your life. When you are young, the path ahead always seems so full of possibilities and fulfilled dreams (and often many of those dreams truly are fulfilled). There are so many

> "Remember also your Creator in the days of your youth, before the evil days come and the years draw near when you will say, I have no delight in them" (Eccl. 12:1).

options available to you as you look to the future, and that carries with it great excitement. You envision graduation, college, a good job, dating, marriage, a house, children, and so on. Or maybe your vision takes you in a different direction. But whatever your future holds, I know that you will take the Lord with you on your journey. Always keep in mind, *"Remember also your Creator in the days of your youth, before the evil days come and the years draw near when you will say, I have no delight in them"* (Eccl. 12:1).

Most of you have obeyed the gospel and have begun your walk as Christians. Teenagers, I admire you so much for that. You have committed to something so great and life-changing at a time when others your age are mired in the physical and the worldly. You have set your mind on things above and made the determination to make those things your number one priority. It is such an inspiration to me and others to think that you could have waited until you had done all the "fun" things that the world has to offer – you could have postponed your commitment to God until after high school, and even college, when it wouldn't seem so important to fit in with friends and classmates. But you didn't do that. Even in your youth, you remembered your Creator. And I don't believe it was simply because you know that life can be short, even for the young. I believe that you truly love the Lord and desire to please Him.

You are involved in so many activities, such as sports, music, and drama to name a few; yet you are all so faithful in your attendance. Yes, I know that your parents have, in most of your cases, always required you to attend. But at some point, that requirement became your own. I have known teenage Christians to be at services when their parents could not. You are at an age where your parents no longer have to push you to do your Bible lessons, for you are diligent about doing them yourselves. I have never taught a high school class, but those who have taught and those who have observed all rave about how well-prepared the students are and how knowledgeable of the material. Your faith has become your own, no longer your parents'. You know why you believe what you believe and are becoming more spiritually mature all the time. That is such a blessing to your parents and to the congregations you attend.

People notice physical changes in you. Your faces still look like your faces . . . yet, they do not. They are different, losing the look of children and transitioning into the faces of a young adults. You are taller, some even taller than me, although that is not really saying much. The boy's voice becomes a man's voice. I know you see these same changes in yourselves, and I know it is exciting for you. But those very changes make this a critical time for you. The world would take your youthful freshness and purity and attempt to sexualize you. Fashion would have you clothe yourselves in revealing outfits, exposing yourselves for the world to see. It flabbergasts me to see the things that some parents allow their teenage girls to wear! But I have been watching the teenagers where I attend and am so proud that they haven't fallen into that trap. They are always stylish, yet modest; and I know it is not always easy to find proper clothing on the racks today. Most Christian teenagers that I know dress in appropriate attire which enhances your inner and outer beauty. A while back we had a young man (going into his last year of high school at the time) hold his very first gospel meeting with us. It was a weekend meeting and his plea to the young women was to dress in such a way that young men would not be tempted to sin when they looked at them. Remember Paul's exhortation to Timothy in 1 Timothy 4:12, *"Let no one look down on your youthfulness, but rather in speech, conduct, love, faith and purity, show yourself an example of those who believe."*

Some of you bring friends to worship from time to time. You are to be greatly commended for that. The services of the Lord's church are very different from what most people are used to, and your friends may think they are too serious or too formal. But you have learned about the authority of the Scriptures and what the church is about – worshipping God. He has given us a pattern to follow, and you know that it is not for our own entertainment but for His glorification. God bless you for your boldness and strength to withstand the lure of the recreational and entertainment activities that so many churches use to entice people to attend.

I appreciate the friendliness of you teenage Christians to everyone in the church. I have known teens who were sullen to the point of rudeness, but you are always smiling and happy to be with the saints of all ages. You don't seem to have the self-absorption that so many teenagers have (~~well, maybe just a little~~). Certainly you enjoy spending time with the other teenagers in the congregation, but you also branch out and remember that we are all part of the same spiritual family. You have so much life and energy and that attracts people to you. I see teenage Christians holding babies, giving the young parents a break. You participate in the social activities that members have in their homes, even to the point of bringing food you made yourself. Your are active members of the church, working in group meetings, cleaning the church building when it is your family's turn, coming to various workdays, going door to door when such evangelistic endeavors are planned. I know you do these things even when you have a mountain of homework at home. This shows your awareness that you have your own place in the congregation, not just as somebody's son or daughter, but in your own right; and you understand the importance of working hard for the Lord.

There are so many other things I could say about you. I want you all to know that I am more proud of you than I can express. You are so vitally important to your congregations. You lift us all in ways that only you can, and I want you to know that you are very much a Barnabas to me!

Deacons

To the faithful, dedicated and hard-working
men serving as deacons, you are a Barnabas to me!
Growing up in the Lord's church, I never really
understood the office of a deacon; and I fear now
that many congregations do not put the necessary
emphasis on the office. Some seem to think they are to
be changers of light bulbs and fixers of clogged sinks.
While there may certainly be some of those types of
things involved, I really can't believe that the Lord
would set down such a list of requirements for this
office just so men can perform these mundane tasks.
In a recent Bible class conducted in our congregation,
we studied the qualifications for those who would be
named to the position of deacons; and a serious set of
qualifications they are. As Paul listed each of them, I
stopped to think of the men of this church who have
been considered by all of our members to fit each one.
I believe that every one of the men accepted the role
with the utmost soberness of mind, knowing that this
was ultimately an appointment sanctioned by God.

Each faithful deacon is grave or dignified. Does
that mean somber, never cracking a smile or showing
a fun side? Certainly not; most deacons I know have
a wonderful sense of humor. But each of you is also

very serious when it comes to the work given to you by God. None of you is double-tongued but honest and respectful in speech. You are not lovers of wine or of money. Each of you is unmovable in regard to sound doctrine, defending the Lord, His gospel, or His church whenever it is called for, and you all have faithful wives and good, obedient children who demonstrate their love and respect for their husband/ father. You provide for your household and are the undisputed head of your home. The Scripture says that *"For those who have served well as deacons obtain for themselves a high standing and great confidence in the faith that is in Christ Jesus."* Does this sound like those who are simply maintenance men and nothing more?

A good group of deacons is an immeasurable help to the elders in devoted performance of their duties. Yes, there is a good bit of taking care of the building and grounds which is absolutely essential, and most work hard at this. But faithful deacons go well above

and beyond those functions. At the congregation I attend, the deacons prepare and update a number of lists. There are lists for duties during the worship services, lists for the group meetings we have every Lord's Day evening, lists for members to help with the mowing and weed-eating in the summer months, lists to pick up members who are unable to drive themselves to services, lists for those who clean the building, lists for classroom teachers each quarter, lists for those who prepare the Lord's Supper trays, and on and on. It boggles my mind. All these lists help the local congregation function as it should.

Recently a newer member of our church family made the comment, "We have the hardest working deacons I have ever seen! It seems like every time I come here, there is a deacon working." Being a deacon can sometimes be a thankless job – a job often taken for granted, if it is thought about at all. It has been a pleasure to dwell on you, to consider your dedicated efforts in bringing our congregation as close to God's plan as you possibly can. Your sacrifices of time, talent, and energy, and the sacrifices of your family in understanding the time it takes to do your work well, encourage every one of us. And as fervently as I can, I declare that you are a Barnabas to me!

Godly Elders

The Lord showed such great wisdom when He created His church. Each facet of it is explicitly authorized through the Scriptures, from its purpose to its function to its worship. And He was very clear when He set forth the organization of the church. I want to focus on devout and godly elders.

> *You have a deeply-rooted love of the Lord and His Word. You make serving Him and keeping the church pure the number one priority in your lives.*

Through the years, I have been part of many different congregations. Some of them had elders; some did not. There is no doubt that, when the church is organized as the Lord desires, it is at its most functional. Business meetings or congregational meetings simply do not allow for the same degree of efficiency and spiritual-mindedness as when there are qualified servants of God leading the flock.

So to all the faithful elders of the Lord's church, I say that you are a Barnabas to me! You have a deeply-rooted love of the Lord and His Word. You make serving Him and keeping the church pure the number one priority in your lives. It is heartwarming to see men of different interests, different backgrounds, and different opinions on many matters be in total harmony when it comes to the church. Obviously that doesn't mean that you agree on every matter that comes along, but your godly attitudes make it possible for you to work through differences of opinions peaceably and with a spirit of love and unity.

When I consider the varying personalities of godly elders, I am proud that you are so humble. I have known churches where there was the scriptural plurality of elders, but in essence only one elder. By that I mean, because one elder was so much more dominant than the others, he made all the decisions

and the others just went along. On the other hand, I have known elderships where little got done because a decision could never be made, either because of stubbornness or simply because they were indecisive men. What a blessing that godly elderships suffer from none of these problems.

Godly elders meet on a regular basis, which in itself is not always done. (This may seem a strange statement, but I have actually known of elders who were constantly out of town seeing no problem with shepherding via cell phones or other electronic devices – impossible!) You are totally focused on the spiritual development of the people of your congregation, because you watch out for their souls. You strive to meet the needs of those who are struggling, whether physically, spiritually, or emotionally, and make sure all in the congregation know that you are available to them. You are open to new ideas (within the realm of Bible authority, of course) and support members who initiate those ideas. It is your every desire that the congregation you oversee should grow, both in number and in spirit.

Scripture is very clear as to how the elders are to lead – not with a heavy hand, but with kindness and love. But at the same time we are warned of wolves from without and within. Having watched godly elders deal with both types of these problems, I applaud your strength and boldness, especially in the face of terrible stress and shameful accusations. Never do you falter; never do you waver in your defense of the truth. And most inspiring of all, never do you retaliate in kind. I don't mean you may have never raised your voice or stood toe to toe against falsehood. But you are scrupulous in not stooping to the level of the wolves.

As an elder's wife and having a "front-row seat" to some of the situations that arise, I also know about the sleepless nights, the floor-walking, the tears, and

the prayers that go into shepherding the flock. You
good men see each and every situation as worthy of
your consideration and notice; again, something that
is not always the case. You know your flock, both their
joys and their hurts, and you are never too proud to
admit your own faults. As a matter of fact, you often
plead for the prayers of the members on your own
behalf. Oh, that that were the case with every man in
this important office! You weep with those who weep
and you rejoice with those who rejoice. A godly elder
is an elder because he wants to serve. You are willing
to make the sacrifice of your time, your energy, and
sometimes your mental peace, to fulfill God's plan for
His church. You are discreet; knowing that the things
told to you in confidence must stay that way.

God expects men of the highest character to be
the overseers of His church. In looking over the list
of qualifications given in 1 Timothy 3 and Titus 1, it
makes me realize how fortunate a congregation is to
have men possessing these critical attributes – men
who willingly undertake the task in all seriousness.
I have heard some crazy things over the years about
elders – I think the worst was that a congregation
appointed a certain man to be an elder "to keep an eye
on him." If that is disheartening to me, I can't begin to
imagine how the Lord must feel.

And I certainly must mention godly wives of elders.
You are so supportive of your husbands, holding up
their hands at all times. You listen, as I do, when he
is worried or hurting over an issue that has arisen.
You pray, as I do, that he will have the wisdom and
strength to deal with problems that come up. I know

you become discouraged, and maybe even angry, as I do, when someone tries to undermine or besmirch his good name. Yet you also realize, as I do, that this office is much bigger than yourselves, so you continually strive to be his helpmeet and his tower of strength. You are godly, intelligent, hospitable women who make the congregation of which you are members better. God bless you for the encouragement (the Barnabas) you are to your husbands and to the church.

> ... I believe that men of great faith accept the challenge because they must. How could they not? By leading the flock, they are obeying God.

Some people may wonder why in the world anyone would choose to be an elder – why would anyone desire this office? Certainly it would be easier to let "someone else" do the job. But I believe that men of great faith accept the challenge because they must. How could they not? By leading the flock, they are obeying God. He is their inspiration to keep going, to keep working, to make this church a light to the world. You lead your congregation; you watch for every member; you appeal to heaven for those you oversee; and it is your most fervent desire that each one of them should be saved. I have heard it wisely said that the office of an elder in the Lord's church is the greatest office in the world, and I believe that. And so, to the wise, respected, and beloved elders, I say from the very bottom of my heart that you are a Barnabas to me!

Preachers

This will be a bit more personal, but I am sure many can identify with what I am writing

Many years ago when I was a young teenager of about 14 or 15, we had a meeting at the church I attended. I can't remember the name of the preacher, but I do remember that he was an older man. (Of course, at that time anyone over 35 seemed older – he was probably younger than I am now!) One evening after the service, he shook my hand as I was leaving and said, "I'll see you again when you've married a preacher." My response to him was, "I guess I'll never see you again!" Well, his words took on a prophetic meaning when several years later I married a preacher.

When we started dating, my husband wasn't even a Christian. But as he began to regularly attend services with me, he started learning. And even though he struggled against it for a little while, his heart was pricked and he obeyed the gospel. That very night he proposed to me. Within a few months he decided that he wanted to spend his life preaching the Word. That older preacher's words came back to me, because I knew that if my husband was going to spend his life preaching, I was going to spend my life as a preacher's wife. So now, here we are 36 years later, still preaching. So to my godly, devoted husband I want to say that you are a Barnabas to me!

When I was growing up in the church, I never spent a minute thinking about what things were like for preachers. We saw them at all the church services, of course, and socially at different times. I never wondered how much time they spent preparing for the sermons and Bible classes, how many private classes they might have been teaching, what stresses or pressures they may have been under as a result of their work, or how much time they were required to spend away from their families. But suddenly, it was the life that we were living – young and admittedly quite naïve though we were.

I never realized how hard a good preacher had to work before I married you. I have watched your strict work ethic over the years, rising every morning (and I do mean EVERY morning) and going to the church building to work. You come home

for lunch, then back you go through the afternoon. I have learned that not all preachers do this, and I partly understand because it can be such a terribly lonely work. It takes a lot of discipline to keep to a rigid schedule when there is no time clock to punch, no supervisor watching, and when you sometimes just don't feel like it. But it has been important to you to put in the time every day for study, prayer, and preparation; you felt that you owed it to the congregation and to your Lord. Your thorough knowledge of Scripture and your well-organized sermons attest to your dedication. Now that our son is also a preacher, I see the same work ethic and the same routines with him. You were a fine example to him of the time an evangelist needs to devote to this essential work. Your hard work inspires me to work harder at whatever I do.

I have seen you deal tactfully with people in some highly stressful situations. I have watched you stay calm outwardly, knowing that you were extremely upset inwardly. You have grown so adept at saying the right things in tense moments and bringing the emotional level to a more manageable state – there is an art to such a thing that shows immense maturity. And while you have many times shown the toll it takes on you when you got home, you managed to at least appear calm when it was needed.

You admit that you are a "numbers guy," and that is definitely the case. It is very hard for you not to measure your success as a preacher with the number of baptisms, restorations, or new members that come. If members become weak and fall away or leave for some other reason, you tend to take that burden upon your own shoulders as a sign of failure on your part, even though nobody else feels that way at all. We live in a time when people don't seem to be looking for the simple gospel anymore. If they are interested in religion at all, it is generally one of the big mega-churches that are so prevalent nowadays, where the members will be entertained and there are no expectations from them. I know this is difficult for all preachers in all areas because it is so hard to find people to teach. I have always felt that one of Satan's greatest tools is discouragement, and I have seen many preachers over the years succumb to these same discouragements and quit. I also know that it has crossed your mind over the years to find a secular job and simply be a member in the pew. But when it came right down to it, you just couldn't stop. You were as Jeremiah, with the word burning in your heart and you could not stay.

You told me once when we were dating that you expected to be a millionaire by the time you reached the age of thirty. That was before you decided to preach! We have definitely been as Paul, learning to live with whatever much or little we received. And we both realize that in this regard we have been blessed with most of the congregations where we have worked, more than some preachers. But I also know that you gave up the retirement plans, the 401K's, and other pension plans that come with secular work, trusting that God would see us through as long as you worked hard and put as much aside as you possibly could. I know you try not to worry about money, but again, you are a numbers guy. I just want you to know that you have been a wonderful provider for your family over the years. We have never had to do without the necessities, even when the money was extremely tight. But a millionaire? No, not by a long stretch. A mansion? Oh, yes, indeed!

I love your boldness in the pulpit, even when you dread the things you have to say. I have seen you wipe your

> " *… you still stand and proclaim what you believe to be the whole counsel of God.*

sweaty palms and take deep breaths before you have risen to speak on those occasions. Everybody wants to be liked, even preachers, and knowing your words will be met with disapproval (or on the rare occasion even outright hostility), you still stand and proclaim what you believe to be the whole counsel of God. This is something I didn't think much about before marrying a preacher. Now I know how much his wife aches for him whenever he is called upon to do this. Whether or not every person agrees with you, the blessed Lord sees your strength. You will be rewarded beyond measure for being a preacher of courage and boldness, as He requires of His proclaimers.

The preaching life can sometimes be a difficult one, but there are also many joys and blessings that come with it. It is so much fun to have a group of preachers come together and tell their stories – I have laughed until I cried at these times. We have made enduring friendships with other preaching couples, as well as faithful members in the churches where we've labored. And I have appreciated the incredibly kind comments that members have said to you over the years; one that really sticks out to me is, "I am glad that my children will hear your preaching as they grow." What an incredible, humbling statement! Faithful members have no idea how much a word of thanks or commendation for a sermon can lift a preacher's spirits.

It has not always been easy, but for 36 years (and counting) you have used your God-given talents for His glory and praise. I am proud to have been the one you chose to be at your side throughout the years. So to you my husband, my friend, my preacher, I declare that you are, and you always have been, a Barnabas to me!

Final Statements

To you friendly brothers and sisters in Christ, you are a Barnabas to me! I have been a visitor at some congregations over the years where I felt invisible because no one even acknowledged my presence. But I have also been made to feel like a VIP just by walking through the door! Friendliness in a congregation cannot be stressed enough, for it may be the initial thing that keeps a visitor coming back. Greeting Who-Knows-Who from Who-Knows-Where is what we should all be doing. I've known some use the excuse of their own shyness or awkwardness stop them from approaching visitors, but I've also seen those same people take a deep breath and break through that barrier. It's one of those things where the more you do it, the easier it becomes. So, to you friendly Christians — you are a Barnabas to me and to everyone else!

> I marvel at the way so many of my faithful brothers and sisters have handled various crises that have befallen you.

I marvel at the way so many of my faithful brothers and sisters have handled various crises that have befallen you. Never once did I see you rail at God or turn your back on Him for the terrible events in your lives. You have cried, oh yes; but you also continued to put one foot in front of the other, even when it was almost too painful to do so, and march on in the trust that He would keep you in His care. I have seen faithful brothers and sisters in Christ pick up the shattered pieces of a life you had expected to live and find a way to create a new life for yourself, and sometimes for your children. Hard times come to us all, but for some of my beloved brethren there have been unimaginable trials. By enduring them with the great faith you manifest, you have shown by example how to live during the lowest of times. Thank you, thank you for your marvelous strength that you have found within yourselves. You are a Barnabas to me!

To married brothers and sisters who have remained faithful and true to your marriage vows over the years, you are truly a Barnabas to me in a world where marriage is under attack from many sides. You are beautiful examples to your children, as well as all of those with whom you come in contact on a daily basis. Your goal is to go to heaven and to help your spouses get there as well. Isn't it lovely to see a couple who has been married for many, many decades continue to show their deep devotion for one another without embarrassment? The world and the church really need to see that. So to all you faithful married couples, please know that you are appreciated beyond measure and I do not take your example for granted. You are a Barnabas to all who know you!

I have been humbled by those of you who have taken a firm stand against sin even when it involved members of your family who were Christians. Over the years I have known Christians, including elders, who were extremely stalwart and steadfast in virtually every doctrinal issue – until it came to their own family members. Suddenly they were hesitant, or just plain unwilling, to do the hard things. But you understand that the very reason God gave the commands He did was to bring them back, not simply to punish them. I can't know the depth of the pain this has caused you, but I know you have cried, prayed, and worried over their souls. You have talked with them, written to them, and pleaded with them to repent. You have backed away from the relationship you once had with them in an effort to help them feel the loss. But what you haven't done is to falter or give in, even when your heart was broken. Oh my dear brothers and sisters, this has to be one of the hardest things for a Christian to do, but it is the step that God requires. Because of your love for Him, you did what was necessary and proved that no family member is more important than true service to God. God bless you for your strength. You are a Barnabas to me!

I know as time goes by I will remember other things that I should have written. In our efforts to remedy issues that may be holding back the congregations we attend, it is easy to overlook the good things. That was my purpose in these writings. Are we perfect? Certainly not. Is there room for improvement? Of course – always. But I love my brothers and sisters who are trying hard to be their best. The life of a

Christian is the best life, but it isn't always easy. Your faith and dedication to our Lord is a glorious testament of true Christianity at work. You are a light in a dark world. You are steady and resolute in your walk with God. You are firm and bold in the proclamation of your hope. You are a Barnabas to me; and it is my prayer that I am a Barnabas to you!

–Vicky Litmer

CPSIA information can be obtained
at www.ICGtesting.com
Printed in the USA
FFHW011251171119
56041510-62001FF